The Secret Story of

Spr

by Jo Ne ...
Illustrated by Humberto Blanco

Contents

OXFORD
UNIVERSITY PRESS

Secret Devices

All around you, every day, there are secret **devices** at work.

They <u>cause</u> your toast to pop up, open your doors, help you sleep well and let you bounce high in the air.

Sometimes you see them, but often you don't. They're coiled up under things and inside things.

What do you think these secret devices are?

'Cause' means to make something happen. What might <u>cause</u> your toast to pop up?

Boing! Boing! Boing! Boing! Boing! Boing!

<u>Welcome</u> to the world of springs! Wide springs, thin springs, long springs, short springs ... The world as we know it wouldn't work without them.

Why does the author say '<u>Welcome</u> to the world of springs'? Does it make you want to continue reading the book?

Springs in Your Home

How many springs have you already used today, without realizing?

It's hard to count. Have you switched on a light? Pushed down the toaster? Pressed a button? All these actions use little springs.

Springtastic fact

There could be over 2000 springs in your home!

Take a look at a door handle. With most doors, you push the handle down to open the door … and the handle lifts back up again by itself.

Inside there's a spring at work. The spring is squeezed when you push on the handle. When you <u>release</u> the handle, the spring returns to its normal shape and pulls the handle back into place.

Push down to squeeze the spring.

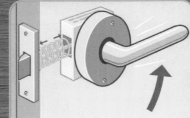

<u>Release</u> to let the spring bounce back.

When you <u>release</u> something, does this mean you hold on to it tightly or that you let it go?

Springs on the Move

There are hundreds more springs in action when you go on a journey. They can be inside, on, or under cars, trains, trucks and bikes.

Many vehicles have large springs above their wheels. These are called 'shock absorbers'. They help to protect the vehicle from bumps, and give you a smoother ride.

As this bike rattles over rocky ground, its springs protect the rider from sudden **jolts**.

Springs are even used in space! For example, they help robotic arms to move.

robotic arm on the International Space Station

How Do Springs Work?

The big <u>advantage</u> of springs is that they don't need batteries or fuel to work. It's their clever shape that allows them to store energy and then release it as they move. When you stretch or squeeze a spring and then release it, it bounces back to its original shape.

An <u>advantage</u> makes something better or more likely to be successful. Why is it an <u>advantage</u> that springs don't need batteries or fuel to move?

How would you <u>describe</u> a spring?

Curled up?   *Round?*   *Spiral-shaped?*

There are actually lots of different shapes of spring, and not all of them are curly or round.

They can be flat, or have bits that stick out, or even be long and thin like a stick.

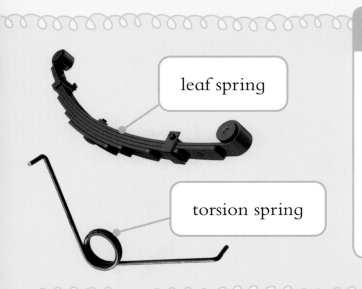

leaf spring

torsion spring

Springtastic fact

The very first springs really were bendy sticks!

Look at the picture of the stick. How would you <u>describe</u> what it looks like?

Early Springs

For many thousands of years, people have used springs to help them <u>survive</u>. The earliest springs were bendy branches made into traps to catch animals for food.

To make the trap, a branch was bent down and cleverly **attached** to a post and a loop of rope. Food was put inside the loop. When an animal came to eat the food, it bumped the trap and the branch pinged up, trapping the animal in the loop.

<u>Survive</u> means to stay alive. What did people do thousands of years ago to help them to <u>survive</u>?

Around 5000 years ago, people started making thin strips of metal into **tweezers**, to grab very small things.

Tweezers have a natural spring in them. If you squeeze them, then release them, they return to their original shape.

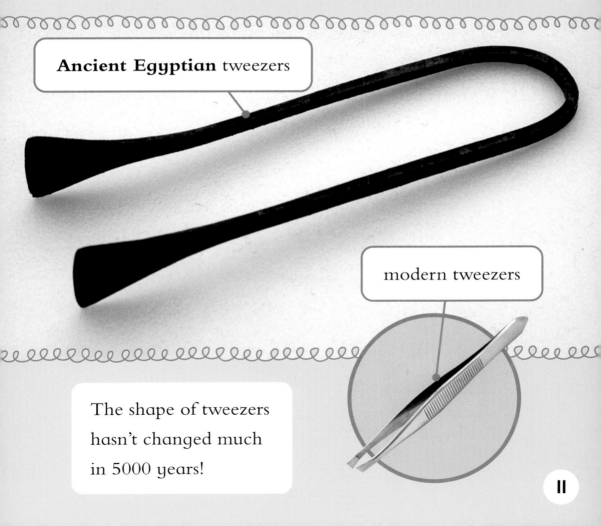

Ancient Egyptian tweezers

modern tweezers

The shape of tweezers hasn't changed much in 5000 years!

Smooth Springs

Over 3000 years ago, the Ancient Egyptians were already using springs in their vehicles.

Travelling on wheels without springs is very uncomfortable. Pharaoh Tutankhamen's (*say fair-oh too-tan-car-mun's*) chariot was built with springy wooden poles attached to the wheels. They protected him from bumps as he sped over rough ground.

chariot

springy poles

Small Springs

About 600 years ago, clockmakers began to power their clocks using springs. They used coiled springs shaped like flat spirals and made from a metal called **steel**.

Before this, clocks had been powered by water or by a swinging pendulum. By using springs, clockmakers could make their clocks a lot smaller than before.

Springtastic fact

A tiny steel spring has enough power in it to keep a clock ticking all day long!

spring inside a modern clock

Bumps and Squeaks

Around 300 years ago, many **carriage**-makers started using 'leaf springs' to make their vehicles travel more smoothly. Leaf springs are made from strips – or 'leaves' – of metal stacked on top of each other.

As the wheels of a vehicle bump up and down, the metal leaves move and bend, which smooths out the bumps and makes the journey more comfortable.

modern leaf spring

You need leaf springs!

leaf spring

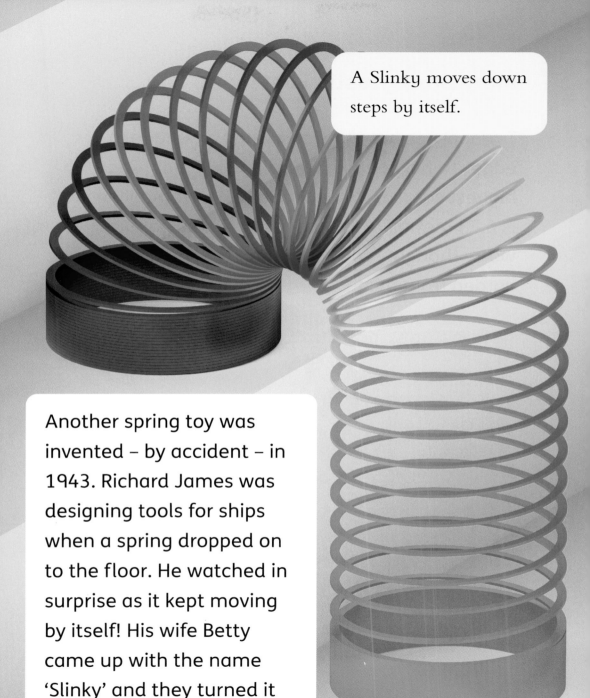

A Slinky moves down steps by itself.

Another spring toy was invented – by accident – in 1943. Richard James was designing tools for ships when a spring dropped on to the floor. He watched in surprise as it kept moving by itself! His wife Betty came up with the name 'Slinky' and they turned it into a bestselling toy.

More Springtastic Facts

Trampolines have lots of springs around their edges to help people to jump really high. The highest someone has jumped on a trampoline is 6.73 metres. That's as high as a house! Don't worry though – you can't jump that high on a garden trampoline.

Springs can also help people survive. Some people have a little machine called a pacemaker fitted inside them. The pacemaker helps to keep their heart beating. Pacemakers work using tiny springs.

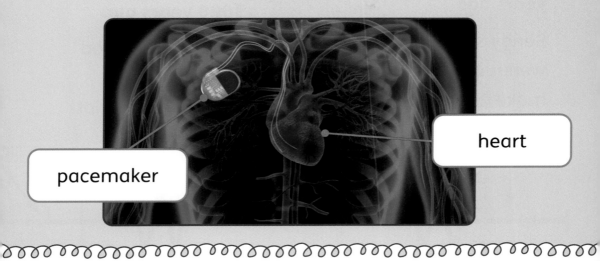

heart

pacemaker

Springs have been making things work for thousands of years. Just imagine what whizzy gadgets they might be used in next!

Springs Through Time

Thousands of years ago

Bendy sticks were used to make animal traps.

3000 years ago

Tutankhamen had springy wooden poles in his chariot.

1500

5000 years ago

Bendy metal strips were used as tweezers.

1430s

The oldest known clock with a spring was made.

1500s

The first jack-in-the-box toys were made.

1763

Tredwell added coiled springs to carriages.

1958

The first pacemaker was given to a patient.

1600   1700   1800   1900   2000

1750s

Leaf springs were used in carriages.

1943

The Slinky was invented.

Glossary

Ancient Egyptian: the Ancient Egyptian people lived in Egypt from around 3100 BCE to 30 CE

attached: fixed or joined on to something else

carriage: a four-wheeled vehicle pulled by horses

devices: things that have been made so that they can do particular jobs

jolts: sudden and rough movements

materials: anything used for making something else, e.g. glass or wool

steel: a type of strong, shiny metal

tweezers: a small instrument like a pair of pincers for plucking out hairs or picking up small objects

Index